A LONG TIME BLOOMING

A LONG TIME BLOOMING

Meditations

MARTA I. VALENTÍN

SKINNER HOUSE BOOKS

BOSTON

www.skinnerhouse.org

Printed in the United States

print ISBN: 978-1-55896-735-9
eBook ISBN: 978-1-55896-736-6

6 5 4 3 2 1
16 15 14

Library of Congress Cataloging-in-Publication Data

Valentín, Marta I.
A long time blooming : meditations / Marta I. Valentín.
    pages cm
  ISBN 978-1-55896-735-9 (pbk. : alk. paper)—
ISBN 978-1-55896-736-6 (ebook) 1. Meditations. I. Title.
  BL624.2.V35 2014
  242—dc23
                        2013049489

For a complete list of meditation manuals, please visit
www.uua.org/skinner/meditation

For Mami and Papi (Marta y Lupito Valentín),
who gave me life and taught me how to live into it.

For Alison and Jaiya,
without whom my life would not be complete.

For Cathy,
who encouraged and held vigil for my heart song.

And for the willing community of
First Church Unitarian in Littleton, Massachusetts,
with whom I walk every day, building the world
we dream about in service and love.

CONTENTS

PREFACE

This is an invitation. A hand extended to welcome you into the world of this Latina lesbian Unitarian Universalist minister—a mouthful no doubt, but it tells you a bit of who I am. The words in this book will tell you a little more about how I live in the world, and how my multiple identities intersect. I hope you will notice that, as seemingly different as some of us may be, there is much about our lives as human beings that serves to connect us.

This is also a gift, a wrapped package to all my fellow Unitarian Universalists whose lives have been marginalized from a lack of cultural and ethical understanding but who nonetheless find the strength every day to remain among us. It is your courage I carry with me as I make this journey too. This book is my act of courage on your behalf that you may feel free to let all of who you are shine forth.

This is also a coming out. One aspect of who I am that has been hardest to live out in this religious movement is my belief in God. As a colleague once said, "I call God, God," and while I have used some metaphors, I did not want to water down my belief, explain it, or qualify it. This book would not be complete without the inclusion of my God experience, which is what has kept me among you.

These words I offer are my heart on paper. The gift of writing given to me, I now share with you. *Gracias*, thank you, for accepting it.

GRATITUDE TO MY ANCESTORS

With honor and respect, these eyes see for you
all manner of life you could not have imagined.
My lips move with the rhythm of your words
flowing through me,
my tongue caressing each morsel of wisdom
I am graced to pass on.
Your DNA rides my veins
and with every breath I take,
your cautious steps from the past
toward a fuller life become
bold moves I make toward my destiny.
Together, we wrap arms
around a new generation,
here to become who they were born to be,
to cast their magic as we once did
and bless each day for their ability to do so.

For you, dear ancestors, we *live* this day.

MAKE NO MISTAKE

Make no mistake about it:
to a certain degree, in certain circles
on gray as well as sunny days,
I am not a free woman in these
un-United States,
and yet, I am more free here
than anywhere else in the world.
Perhaps free is not the right word;
perhaps liberated is more exact.
I am not entirely free for I represent
too many targets as a person of color, lesbian,
a woman from the barrios of Spanish Harlem. . . .
Sometimes though, I *think* I am safe because I was
born on this soil.
The truth is
my body manifested in New York City,
but my soul, *mi corazón*, gave birth to itself
in Puerto Rico.

My own revolution: I fight the world within
that aches and prays for solace and resolution,
and I fight the world without that hammers every
day at my cultural armor as it strives to break me
down, cell by cell, that I might re-emerge united
and in the state of assimilation.

Instead, I rise and make my own religion because
I can do that here.
Basket in hand I set about groping and smelling
for the spirits and the spiritual; shopping in
alleys, mosques and malls
I mix together the salves that will restore
my cultural armor to a *spic* and span glow.
I gather prayers, *refránes*, and my godchild's
smile, which become my walking stick
when I cannot see,
the faith that sheds light on the darkest parts.
I make my religion with the light and the dark
and the hope that the two together
will keep me whole.

Standing before my altar I pay homage
to the fact that I *do* have choices,
too numerous to name in this space.
So, I make sure to account for
every act of free will I am graced with,
knowing that others are not.
I make sure to give thanks for the gift
of putting words on a page,
knowing that others cannot.
I make sure to speak with love,
and to love, with grace.

corazón: heart
spic: derogatory term for a Latino or Hispanic person
refránes: refrains or sayings

ESPERANDO

Entra aquí en el centro,
    ven desde los márgenes,
que aquí te consuelo.

No mires atrás,
    ni a tu alrededor—
el agua está subiendo;
    siente mis brazos abrigándote
mientras tiemblas.
Yo te calentaré.

No mires afuera,
    ni a la lejanía
que la vida está aquí
    entre tú y yo.

En este espacio diminuto
donde yo termino y tú comienzas,
    vive la esperanza.

En este precioso espacio pequeñito,
no hay que susurrar palabras
diciéndonos que somos uno.

Tú y yo
    formamos el círculo
si lo elegimos.

Ven,
　　acércate:
te estoy esperando.

Traducido por Lilia Cuervo y Marta Valentín

WAITING

Step into the center
    come in from the margins
I will hold you here.

Don't look back
      or around
feel my arms
    the water is rising.
I will hold you
as you tremble.
I will warm you.

Don't look out
      or away
life is in here
    between you and me.

In this tiny space,
where I end and you begin
    hope lives.

In this precious tiny space
no words need be whispered
to tell us we are one.

You and I
      we make the circle
if we choose to.

Come
      step in
I am waiting for you.

A CALL TO ARMS

(prayer)

Spirit of Truth and Justice,
hear us as we ask that You hold
the collective anxiety that permeates
this community today. This
is a call to arms. Arms that will hold those with
broken or elated hearts, arms that will wrap
themselves around beaten bodies, battered souls;
arms stronger than either giver or receiver knows,
arms that keep the weight of misplaced
authority and righteousness from crashing down
upon those struggling to hold their heads high
as each shred of dignity is yanked
from their over-used, under-appreciated bodies.
This is a call for committed arms,
and minds and hearts that know the facts
but feel the truth, a call to remember
that the freedom we've been given to swing
our arms as wide and open to the sun as we like
has come on the backs of human beings
others wish were invisible.
This is a call to arm ourselves
with the facts *and* feel the truth
borne out of the power of our
Unitarian Universalist love,
and the balance of justice.

THEOLOGICAL TOURIST

I have come to you on my knees Cuba,
but I am not sure that I have prayed.
I have come to wonder Cuba,
if your churches are helping
out of charity or justice?
If everyone is hungry including your priests,
ministers, and multitudes of lay women,
how do you replenish souls?
Can you break bread and feed your masses?
Can you break dogma to make your bread?
Your children call Obátala,
your children call Jesus,
while sitting next to one another in the pews.
Will God and the Pantheon save you?
I think you seek the kingdom by way
of the revolving door
between your country and mine,
but when I look into your eyes,
it is "just" survival that looks through me.
Your dignity raises the hair on the back of my neck
with its tenacious assertion.
Sing hallelujah.
Sing to any God or deity
that will hear your petitions.
Hosanna in Cuba, as it is in the United States.
Blessed are you who come in the name of Love.

Heaven and earth are filled with all of our glories.
Hosanna in the highest good
for all of God's people . . .

This I see and hear and feel as I pass,
looking through the bus window.

THE CHOSEN

It was the Jazz and Heritage Festival that first brought me to New Orleans. The weekend of fantastic music and food was soul-inspiring.

Seven years later, I have moved to New Orleans, and it is Mardi Gras time. Two weeks after arriving, Hurricane Katrina was lapping at my heels, and now, the first post-flood Mardi Gras is happening. I am not sure what to expect. Outside of the Crescent City, people think the city is wasting what little resources it has. But inside, everyone feels Mardi Gras is needed to lift our spirits.

At eight o'clock in the morning, I go to Lee Circle dressed as a refrigerator (like so many that lined the streets for months), with my outlaw of a wife dressed in a bathrobe and curlers. It's hot and humid and folks are lining up to watch the parades all day. Couches are on the curb, grills are fired-up, ice chests are filled to the brim, and modified ladders with seats on top for small children are installed—primo spots to catch the prizes thrown from the floats.

The parade rolls, and the frenzy begins as onlookers rush the floats in hopes of getting a coveted painted coconut from Zulu, the only all-Black krewe.

At first I stand back and watch. I am enthralled by it all. Here what I experience is not the drunken craziness the news media like to call Mardi Gras. Here what I experience are families and strangers sharing their food and drink, children darting around picking up beads and candies that slip through hands. In a flash, I too am out in the street jumping.

Suddenly I realize that Mardi Gras is all about *being seen*. Of the thousands of folks lining the sidewalks, every one wants to be seen, every one wants to be chosen. Magic happens when eyes lock, and the masked person looks at *you* to throw *you* a gift. And I realize too that the thrill of being seen is why Mardi Gras will always go on. That intimate moment of eyes meeting and gifts being tossed brings new meaning to "Me, pick me!"

We all want to be seen and spend lifetimes attempting to achieve it. The Mardi Gras season gives us innumerable opportunities to do just that, as addiction to fleeting moments leaves us with beads and trinkets. But if you are as lucky as I was, you may bring home a coveted painted coconut to remind you of that moment in time when someone saw you and chose you.

THROUGH THE WINDOW

(post-Katrina)

I watch her sitting on a plastic crate
as she sorts through, cleans and keeps
or discards the pieces of our life
that remain from the disaster.

Memories laid out on the asphalt drive—
she barters with the sun
to dry and burn the mold away,
the black and smelly animal that clings to all,
obscuring the clear view of a past that was once
ours.

Does she cry when no one is watching?
Does she doubt herself for clinging, mold-like,
to a kind of past
that will never be again?

By what criteria does she decide
what will go into our future with us?
Through the window, I watch my love
attempt to scrub away our sorrows as if
tomorrow will not bring more.

Through the window, I watch my love
and my heart sings
for a life of blessings with her
that I have lived with no other.

COMING CLEAN

is another way of finding peace in one's heart.

It is looking up at the clear crisp lavender sky
to find a reflection of my soul spelling out God's
prayer among the wisps of clouds—
"Love thyself and then you will truly love me. . . ."

Coming clean does not
wipe out imagined slates of guilt and suffering,
does not imply traveling a continuum from evil
toward what is good, blessed, pure, untarnished. . . .

To come clean
is what pounds in my heart,
inviting me into its rhythms,
inviting me to create music out of cacophonous
sounds and dance from beats richly textured
and interwoven by:
Faith,
Hope,
Love. . . .

I am coming clean
as the droplet pearls from God's own forehead
bless and sweat with me, as I wash away layers
of disillusioned grime, disheartened dirt, crimes
of passion committed against my own heart.

I am coming clean
because I want to go.
I am tired of standing still
mistaking a quiver and a quake
for truthful movement.

I am coming clean
so that I can say I have come clean.
To you, to me, and to this life.

JOURNEY THROUGH LIGHTNESS

There are times in your life
when you will light many candles at once
under the pretense of illuminating someone else's
world
but actually only to illuminate your own. . . .
Or perhaps for some variety
(and peace of mind and heart),
you will light one candle at a time
one right after the other
or spaced out to allow
for a shift in wind. . . .
Then there are times, of course,
when you will light no candle
and favor sitting alone,
letting the darkness fall around you,
inside you,
sometimes on top of you. . . .
Rest assured, though,
that somewhere
in your journey through lightness
there will be one candle
that will not extinguish itself
and remain spiritually lit.

BE STILL WITH ME AND ENTER

(call to worship)

Be still with me and enter
into the crescent fold of my arm
as I gather you to this time and space.
Wind your thoughts like a river
toward the center of who we are:
this morning as one body, and out among
others in the world.
Be still with me and enter into this celebration
of resilience and resurrection.
For we are vessels eternally rising
out of the water,
alive
with a purpose and strength unknown to us.
Be still with me and enter, quietly,
into this place of unbound love and gratitude.

EARTHQUAKE

(Ahmedabad, India, 2001)

Mother Earth is shouting
but we do not hear.
She is filled with anguish,
for all we understand
is death.
And in her agony
she suffers too over the fact
that she must kill
her own
to get our attention.

DOÑA LEO

If Mother Earth walked among us she would
have the young yet ancient face of Doña Leo,
her long gray-white braids gentle on each breast,
like roots pointing toward the ground.

She would rise quietly so as not to wake the sun,
bless herself facing the four directions,
offer her soul in gratitude to the One who is,
and go about feeding the children of everywhere.

With the grace and flexibility of a flower bowing
in the wind, she would gather corn for tortillas,
the Holy Eucharist of the indigenous people.
Beyond the body of Christ, it is
the body of the Mexican people,
that body that struggles every hour
to be fed, nurtured, nourished,
to be fortified, enriched, empowered. . . .

We come and she will feed us, humbly hiding herself
in her kitchen sanctuary,
where something simple and grand is made
from nothing.
Eventually she will re-appear
like *La Virgencita*
with love and the beginning of time
reflected in her eyes.
This time she will offer her healing touch.

Hands that pick coffee and corn
rub limbs, backs, and foreheads gently
with homemade salves passed down
through generations of *curanderas*,
every sinew and muscle blessed
by Doña Leo and all her elders before her.

Her language is in her hands,
preferring to act rather than speak.
Her love is in her hands,
preferring to give rather than take away.
Her God is in her hands,
preferring to heal rather than harm the earth,
her brothers and sisters,
but most importantly, the next generation.

La Virgencita: The Virgin Mary
curandera: healer

MERIDA, VENEZUELA

As I sit on the edge of this Andean mountaintop,
across the valley farmers tend
to their seemingly vertical gardens as sounds
echo and bounce off the vegetation.
Laughter rings the bowl of mountains,
when families greet each other as they pass,
making the slow trek up into the heavens.
The sun begins its descent and white billowy
clouds slowly roll in, like a curtain of angel
gowns floating and swirling as tree tops
disappear, then houses, huts, and bushes.
Even sounds of barking dogs fade into the
ground as a celestial paradise envelops me.
There is nothing to do but lay back
on the wet grass, arms and legs stretched wide
and sing praises for the divine glory
of this magnificent earthly experience hidden
in the clouds.
Then, there is nothing to do but turn over and,
prone, kiss the earth
in blessing for holding us all.
Then, there is nothing to do but stand,
hands in prayer held to heart,
in infinite gratitude for the gift of sight.

Behold, this majestic mountain in heaven and
just below it.
As the misty night approaches,
I am lost in the clouds but have found in my soul
a memory I did not know I had.

THE GOLDEN PRESENT

. . . is not like the proverbial egg that expects
you to sit on it and wait. . . .
It is instead a scrumptious feast
to be served when you call.
Look around, it awaits a response from you,
one that says:
"Yes, I see you,
Yes, I choose you,
Yes. . . ."

The golden present ever reaches for you
and wonders if you'll come
to unwrap its gifts.

LIVING PRAYER

You are my living prayer
but I do not kneel before you
to speak your name
or make supplications. . . .
I walk beside you,
two seekers on the journey,
soft chants of love beneath our breaths,
lifelines pressed together;
we move forward toward
each other.

LISTENING FOR YOUR WORD

(prayer)

Spirit of all Lives,
You hold in your heart and hands
all that is good and just, as you wait
for us to grab and take hold.
Teach us to know when to reach,
and when to release, when to pray,
or when simply to stand still
listening for your word.
Teach us to trust that what we hear
is not our imaginations,
and help us to accept this.
Spirit of my Life, guide me this day
as I open the path before me
with you as my beacon,
my light, the star whose glow I follow.
Amen and Blessed Be.

A SYMPHONY OF VOICES

(*Bridging litany*)
*Spanish speaker,   **youth

Voice 1:	Wherever it is we are going,
Voice 2*:	the reality is that we *are* going! *¡Vamos!*
Voice 3**:	Into a soul-inspiring life
Voice 4:	to have & create beloved communities
Voice 5:	where we can be who we are,
Voice 3:	however we are, speaking the language
Voice 4:	of our hearts and our heritage
Voice 5:	so that more than *feel* like we belong
Voice 2:	*sabemos*, we *know* we do
Voice 1:	when we are honored and sought after
Voice 3:	for our gifts, knowledge, and wisdom.
Voice 5:	We desire to walk with our communities as they walk with us.
Voice 3:	In crossing over into young adulthood
Voice 4:	we find vulnerability on either edge
Voice 5:	so we place stones before us as we make our way toward building
Voice 2:	*una comunidad*, a community
Voice 3:	generated out of love and compassion,
Voice 4:	trust and friendship,
Voice 2:	*fe en las posibilidades*, faith in the possibilities,
Voice 1:	and new discoveries that create fearlessness out of a holy curiosity.
Voice 5:	We are you, and as such

Voice 3:	we are your legacy.
Voice 5:	You may not know me, but think of me
Voice 4:	and every child you meet as your legacy.
Voice 2:	And when you do, think of how you will work with us toward a just future.
Voice 3:	A future we will be proud to pass on to the bridgers of tomorrow.
Voice 5:	We are wise enough to know that the youth we leave behind
Voice 3:	like me are *our* legacies.
Voice 1:	So, as we move forward, we place stones down behind us as well
Voice 4:	that they may find their way,
Voice 1:	that they may know there is a solid foundation for them to walk on
Voice 2:	into the young adulthood community of love that awaits them.
Voice 3:	As we build the bridges to our futures,
Voice 1:	we are mindful that they will be held together
Voice 2:	by our passion for each other, the world,
Voice 5:	and this beautiful faith we call Unitarian Universalism, which ever asks of us
Voice 4:	to build the most important bridge of all,
Voice 1:	the one called relationships,
Voice 2:	kinship, *familia*,
Voice 3:	the one that tells us who we are by which relations matter.
Voice 5:	I am you and invite you to be me
Voice 2:	and build this bridge together.

NOTHING TO FEAR

Go forth, young child, and know
that you do not walk alone,
nor ever have.
You carry with you ancestral bonds
that do not sever.
You carry with you familial love
that does not end.
You carry with you
the scents of sweet friendships
a long time blooming. . . .
Go forth, young child,
with nothing to fear.
Open your heart
to the crosscurrents of living.
Let others enter the circle
of your tender loving arms.
Let others know the profundity
of your sharp, inquiring mind.
Go, leave your mark upon the world,
and continue to lift up your voice,
there are many waiting to listen.

. . . KNOWS NO BOUNDS

You must live and breathe
it must be the first thought in the morning and
the last at night, when twilight descends.
It must be what you search for in the darkness,
the light that leads you to find who you are,
where you are, what you are. . . .
It is understood already that you would die for it,
but would you be willing to be born again for it?
Change your cells for it?
If you were dying of thirst,
it would be your only drink of water,
the one liquid to quench your thirst,
sate your parched soul,
resuscitate your empty lungs.
In the dead of winter, it will be your fire, blanket,
scarf, and hat.
In the desert, it would be your mirage and
your oasis.
Even when you don't want it, can't stand it, despise it—
it will come looking for you, haunt you,
track you down,
beg your attention and your love.
For the purpose that you were blessed with
knows no bounds,

only that if you are not paying attention,
you will be lost until it finds you,
until you heed its call and be who and what
you were meant to be.

CHILDREN OF YOUR LIGHT

(GLBTQ prayer)

Mother Father God,
we have emerged as a world of rainbows
in your magnificent image
and we sing our praises in your honor.

Mother Father God,
there are many in our communities
who are lost, hurt, and dying.
There are many who dare not speak,
many who speak and are not heard,
many who wish to speak and have no words.
Help us all, queer and non-queer,
to gather this day, worship together,
sit at the table as one, and break
not only bread but misconceptions.

In this world,
which daily challenges our existence,
our interior rock that allows us to hold
our ground
enlarges with every resolution
to speak on your behalf,
to honor the divinity within ourselves,
and to give witness as children of your light.

ELEMENTAL

In the evening you are
air,
deep breaths that free you
from the earthly day,
wind that travels through the night,
through all worlds,
currents starting in the mind
and ending in the morning,
where you are
water
seeking water, parched lips and dry throat
with hot streams of wetness.
Streaming eyes and steaming mirrors
bring you nearer to the
earth,
where you labor, toil, and struggle,
slip through another hour,
push through another day,
steady aiming for the evening air,
to free you, feed you, and remind you:
that in the loving you are
fire,
any love that it may be,
you bring warmth, light and healing
to the day the light of truth

to the night the warmth of trust
and in the dew the healing touch
and to the love, to the love
the fire that is you
brings hope to hearts untrue
and seeds the world anew.

MY NATURE WALK

As a "real" Unitarian Universalist,
I feel that I should be writing about nature.
Something about trees and rivers,
or tiny slugs on dahlias munching away
with their hundreds of thousands of teeth,
wreaking havoc in my non-existent garden.
Or maybe about how I get lost in the woods
I never actually venture into alone
because to a city girl, they are really scary,
with foreign, unidentifiable sounds,
not like the knowing rumblings
of a yellow taxi passing me by
in the middle of the night
or the rattle of the train under my feet.

The kind of nature I want to tell you about
is often disguised as culture. . . .
the culture of a people and place and
the nature of a people and place are to me
one and the same.
The indigenous nature of my people is actually
quite comfortable in the woods.
The African culture of my people
is colored by their roots in the Motherland.
The Spanish in my people
likes to mess with the culture of those
they want to conquer.

(I still have some forgiveness to work on with
that part of my culture.)
And sometimes, when I go out for a nice, long
"nature" walk, I think about that
while I try to make out how my nature
and the Unitarian Universalist culture can
co-exist, each complete unto itself yet
forming a third space together.
Will it be a natural place to be
or a contrived cultural creation?

The nature of this particular search for
truth and meaning requires
a cultural adaptation
that I might walk free, whole, and complete.

RACIAL ELIJAH

We gather in places made sacred
by our witness to each other's presence.
Yet the sacredness is incomplete:
There is a hole so evident and so large that
it is not seen because we look right through it.
We barely see the edges of its existence when
we look only to the faces entering
that reflect our own.
The other is hardly missed when the welcome
mat is taken up and shaken of its dirt.
The hole persists.
The chair remains empty, an unseen gift,
and the black and white world
remains just that.
And yet, I too am here, sitting in the circle.
Am I the only one noticing who is not here?
Am I the only one craving to fill the circle?
Am I the only one?

Sometimes,
I feel like a racial Elijah
listening for God's whispers
to help make sense of it all.

EMBRACING MY CULTURES

begins with every Puerto Rican bowl
of rice and beans I feed my body
that gives sustenance to my soul,
like the Latin rhythms that stem
from the "I" of my heart.

It continues lavishly garnished with
GLBT rainbow spices,
and a side of feminist fierceness,
which insists on the "yes!" of my life.

Then, it all comes together at the
Unitarian Universalist table where, as a
minister, I am careful to be authentically,
multi-culturally, inclusive.

In order for me to *be* me,
I must embrace all my cultures and
simply ask the same of you.

PER"SPIC"TIVE

is seeing my Latin sisters and brothers
day in and day out being trampled on
judged by systems we don't understand
and that don't have an interest in understanding us
because we don't speak the language
haven't learned to play the games
don't care to step on others
as a ladder to a higher hell. . . .

We are not victims, mind you
we just have a different per"spic"tive
on what living is
knowing what it's like
to be the walking dead.
We don't strive to own three cars,
we struggle for the chance
to see our homelands again. . . .

We are not interested in knowing our neighbors
to compare material gains,
but instead to relieve spiritual pains.
Our children walk the same way to school
but once they pass the threshold
the paths diverge,
the good to the right
all others to the left.
It used to be Johnny couldn't read

now it's Juan and Maritza
with language the easy excuse
for the barrier. . . .

Yes, our per"spic"tive is quite different
I wouldn't say unique, or even special,
but it is our own
one that we cherish
and struggle to maintain
as we are bombarded
by what the dominant culture demands:
our children and grandchildren
believing it so as to *feel* like they belong,
insisting,
it is the only way to survive, be heard,
understood. . . .

But, having lost their per"spic"tive
they know not what they say. . . .

SELF-*ISH*

Unless you were of a certain shade
and persuasion
you were not taught by the world
outside of your family
that what you thought mattered,
that how you showed up in the world
could alter the real in reality,
that who you loved
would bring to light forms of affections
always present, yet kept in darkness.

To bring value back to your
Self
in a world that functions by daily
stripping you of it,
you must hold fast to being
first
in your mind and heart.
To be number one
to number one,
means being self-*ish*, that is, knowing
that who and what you have been
in spite of the intrusion and institution
of internalized oppression
makes all the difference
in creating a multicultural world
and must shine forth.

CHORDS OF RIPENING WISDOM

(for Audre Lorde, Elizabeth Schussler Fiorenza, and Rita Nakashima Brock)

The first question, at least for today, is:
How do I construct a theology without
a truth-filled history?

Audre tells me that I *cannot* dismantle
the Master's house using the Master's tools. To
attempt to uncover who my God is with tools
designed to exclude me is to pretend that I am
blind while born with perfect sight,
is to forsake *self-understanding* that I might see
like others.

Elizabeth tells me to *use* the Master's tools to
dismantle the Master's house. But without a
manual I can spend a lifetime
barreling through the front door with a log
simply because it is *there*.
Yet I know that same log can only break down
back doors to ensure *my*
survival.

No more.

In search of *wholeness*, I wonder if the answer
is to use new tools to create a new house?
Or do we get rid of the house

by getting rid of the tools?
It is clear that the Master must go,
but should a Mistress move in?

My answer lies in Rita's tribal consciousness of
self-understanding, survival, wholeness. . . .
In creating, building, discovering,
out of this world's cacophonous madness, I can be
guided through a self-governing tribe of voices
that crescendo into chords of ripening wisdom,
each with its own melody.

I can have a center, a flexible observer who can
listen beyond hearing,
reflect beyond seeing,
choose beyond settling.
And in this way constantly reconstruct meaning.

BLOOMING IS YOUR WAY

Daddy, this is your girl here.
I've climbed down off Your knee
with a sack of *isms* and *archys* on my back
ready to crawl the land.
Skirting tax collectors and roadside lame
I crawl along, cloak-free, sandal free,
sacred oil in my satchel.
I crawl in search of what is mine.
I know You put it here somewhere,
although my brothers
have masked your intentions. . . .

Still, I am here
as You, Abba, ever will be
for You and I, we are One.
And while You are Daddy,
I ain't nobody's mammy, and what is done to me,
withheld from me,
hidden from me,
is done, withheld, and hidden from You too.
Lost, we search for Your good Graces in
every garden, under every rock,
behind every bush, burning or not, but never,
in our own mirrors.

I'm here Daddy, right where you planted me
and I will bloom as flowers often do
in the tiniest of sidewalk cracks. . . .
I will bloom.
I have bloomed.
For blooming is Your way.

TO BE SEEN

What began as wisps turned into clouds
and eventually curtains of smoke,
thick and opaque with no light for reflections,
smokescreens created to deny you,
the smiling truth teller (who has no bounds
when voicing God's words),
the spirit dweller (who fills each empty space with love),
the soul stirrer (who moves to all rhythms
with or without sound).

Wise shaman, the smoke is dissipating,
revealing the gifts
that you must always offer without shame.
Your gifts inspire, breathe life into both
the living and the living dead,
the conscious and the unconscious,
the initiated and the uninitiated.

Your spirit and soul are calling to be whole
and it is no accident.

Let yourself be restored once again
as God sweetly, proudly, places a gentle kiss
upon your forehead to anoint you

And as I celebrate you, I grieve too
the loss of our own dream of working together
to bring to life a multicultural, justice-making
community of hope, where
all are seen,
all are heard,
all are touched in love, not fear.

Go forward my friend
into your destiny. Let yourself be held
as you have held so many others
now that you are finally being seen.

PRAYER FOR PEACE AND HEALING

Spirit of Life all around us
You have gathered us together
in a swirl of healing wind. . . .
Take this newfound apprehension,
an unwelcomed shawl
heavy upon our shoulders
and make of it a comforter
soft and warm and trusting
in which we might rest our weary souls. . . .

Each day we awaken
may our first thought and vision
be the peace in the eyes
of our sisters, brothers, cousins,
who also see the peace in mine.

And from this gaze into each other,
may the peace of our hearts
heal one another.

A LASTING CLOTH

There are many things that I can hold:
I can hold your exhausting pain on my lap
as you free yourself for a moment of respite. . . .

I can hold your unspeakable sorrow in the crevices
of my arms as I would a nascent babe,
tenderly and carefully.

I can hold your eyes open, gently, with the
tips of my fingers as you fight to stay awake,
never missing one minute.

I can hold the pieces of your heart, mindful
not to lose any one in a careless moment,
mindful that you will need them all back
when you are able to stop gasping and
take deep breaths again.

I can hold you up walking beside you,
a human staff to lean on when your weakened
knees buckle predictably,
as you fight the urge to crawl.

But the one thing I cannot hold,
for it is too large to grasp,
is the sudden hole that has rent
the fabric of your life.

Now you must find a way to hold it
when you begin to weave your life anew.
I pray that in time you can overlap
strand upon strand
of the love that surrounds you
into a lasting cloth that will ever hold you.

TO KNOW SUCH LOVE

To be so blessed with an open heart
that the adoration of a furry being
could easily penetrate,
curl up and purr within it.

To be so blessed with an open mind,
to believe that friendship and
companionship, unconditional and complete,
is possible, perhaps even a necessary
prelude
to accepting human affection in its vast capacity.

To be so blessed with an open spirit
and understand
that a hand stroke for one
is a lap nap for another;
the silent way
one expresses such ardor
that has no name
lives in its own realm, and is
given only to those willing to engage
in the fullness of God's offerings.

I have been so blessed
to know such love
because
I have known you.

REMEMBRANCE COMES

(for Papi)

At rest with the dying,
our mutual immortality
is stirred.

As his new awakening approaches,
one that we have forgotten would come,
my eyes grow dim and sleepy,
pulled by gravity.

But when we are laying side by side
lost in earth's weariness,
me on my back,
him in a fetal position,
the completeness of the reality
that my final awakening
will some day come too,
leads me to embrace my child
in a way he could not his own
until my forty-first year,
transforming the once held longing
for affection
into an accepted gratitude.

And it is then
that remembrance comes
and liberation is welcomed.

IN EVERY DEATH

It has been said
that in every death
we lose a little
of who we are.

A relationship with our
self is severed
and bereft
we are left to re-discover,
re-imagine, then
re-select
who we came to be.

BEGINNING AGAIN ON THE CONTINUOUS
JOURNEY

By the *grace* of the Divine Power,
which is larger hearted than we can ever imagine
we are constantly given the opportunity
to begin again
as the signposts along the continuous journey
suggest twists and turns we had not brought into view,
for the focus was on the mountains just up ahead
beyond the ridge. . . .

By the *faith* of the Divine Power
that lives through the trust of our human ability
we are constantly offered the challenge to test the waters,
not just smooth the inevitable ripples
to a satiny gloss finish as if
that were the goal in life,
losing all character by not realizing:
the swells are what make life
interesting, intriguing, and indescribable.

By the *love* of the Divine Power,
whose very core is compassion
for our earthly missteps on this journey,
we are constantly given an opening

to remember that we each have a place
in the kin-dom* of humanity,
and the knowledge
and courage to begin again toward a faith-filled,
loving grace that is our birthright.

*from Ana Maria Isasi-Diaz

THE ONE TRUE RESPONSE

Life has been doing itself since it was created.
In the beginning, as it is now,
it has been about becoming. . . .
What does the world wish to become?
Its magical secrets hidden among the leaves in the
forest—sitting, waiting, being, yearning
to be discovered by a fellow traveler. . . .
Desiring to be, the world has been surrounded,
cornered, encroached upon by an army of doers,
relentlessly testing reality,
the sin of simply standing there like a forest tree
unbearable,
unimaginable,
yet inevitable,
a necessary rite of passage requiring
only movement of the mind. . . .
Spirit teaches every day that the act of doing
is based on being: they are inextricable.
In the being, the leaf falls gracefully
to float along on the wings of wind,
letting itself rest on the forest floor
or be held by another branch,
letting itself move downstream
trusting the process, remembering that Spirit is the host
and the leaf a guest in this life,
knowing in its being that its story

is its own history of salvation,
even amidst a million leaves in the forest.

God calls. . . .
    Spirit calls. . . .
        Life calls. . . .
and the act of being is the one true response.

MOONSHINE

People of the rich and dark night:
rise up,
come out into the light.
Let the glow of the most holy moon
embolden the you that is You,
to shine forth with your hues and your blues,
extending the moon's hallowed halo
out to the edges of this sacred universe
where beloved inclusion transcends space,
race, and time,
defying the weight of gravity,
which fights to hold us in place.
Don't let it.
Propel your Selves forward
by the strength, and the force
of this collective love roaring in your heart,
that the world may be enchanted,
by your song of ten thousand languages
in its polyrhythms and mega-forms,
until the message of this global majority
is heard.

UNITARIAN UNIVERSALIST MEDITATION MANUALS

Unitarians and Universalists have been publishing prayer collections and meditation manuals for more than 170 years. In 1841 the Unitarians broke with their tradition of addressing only theological topics and published *Short Prayers for the Morning and Evening of Every Day in the Week, with Occasional Prayers and Thanksgivings.* Over the years, the Unitarians published many more volumes of prayers, including Theodore Parker's selections. In 1938 *Gaining a Radiant Faith* by Henry H. Saunderson launched the tradition of an annual Lenten manual.

Several Universalist collections appeared in the early nineteenth century. A comprehensive Book of Prayers was published in 1839, featuring both public and private devotions. Like the Unitarians, the Universalists published Lenten manuals, and in the 1950s they complemented this series with Advent manuals.

Since 1961, the year the Unitarians and Universalists consolidated, the Lenten manual has evolved into a meditation manual.

For a complete list of meditation manuals, please visit
www.uua.org/skinner/meditation